#relatable

#relatable

Written by Marquita Norwood

Illustrations by Marquita Norwood

Cover design by Axel Van Zyl

#relatable

Copyright © 2018 by Marquita Norwood

All rights reserved.

ISBN-13: 978-1986356305

ISBN-10: 1986356302

Contents

Just Throw the Whole Brain Away 13
Wild Thots...................................22
Memoirs of a Gangsta 35
Boycott Feelings............................ 40
Send Nudes..................................47
Have You Tried Not Being Depressed? 54

I dedicate this book to my friends and social media followers who largely encouraged its publication. All proceeds will directly support my charcuterie addiction. I love you all. Almost more than prosciutto. Almost.

TESTIMONIALS OF MARQUITA NORWOOD

"When Marquita's eyebrows aren't launching the fleet of a thousand ships, she is making observations about the world which are by turns hilarious and wonderful; often both. Her wit, supreme as it is, is matched only by her kindness. I am very British so you have to believe me."

—Sarah-Louise Jordan, very British

"Marquita? Now that's a bad bitch. Wittiest mothafucka I ever met. Oscar Wilde whomst? Gorgeous smile. Have me cracking up for days! When she finally learns to lay a wig correctly and boost her credit score, it's over for you hoes."

—Zora Neale Twurksumn, fellow bad bitch

"Marquita (Sade? Norwood? YOU DECIDE) is the funniest person I know, and I regularly doubt my own comedy skills because of her."

—Samantha Irby, author of *We Are Never Meeting in Real Life*

"Marquita is better than you at *everything*. She's the kind of hilarious that has nuance. The way she interprets the world and uses nostalgia to create memes is extraordinary. Oh, and her cheekbones can cut glass."

—Siete Saudades, Clapback King

"Marquita is a part of my morning routine; wake up, shower, shave, get my wig *snatched* by Marquita's content. This bitch be having my lace front flapping in the wind like I'm a bald eagle. She'll hit me with jokes so powerful they gotta perform last rites. She's a force to be reckoned with."

—Kenji, Mrs. Karabayeva if you nasty

> **Hey Big Head.**

This is mostly a book for bored millennials who ran out of things to watch and memes weren't enough. Also if you're reading this, so like what are we?

#relatable

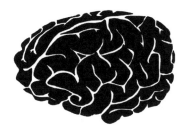

Just Throw the Whole Brain Away

You wonder why we all got issues with self-identity and image when the mirror; the front cam; the back cam; the webcam and a car window all make us look mad different. Are we servin' face or disgrace? What is the actual truth? What the fuck do we look like?

***

You'll be having a good morning until you have to solve for x 'cause you're tryna take a shower at somebody else's house. After 20 minutes of tryna turn on a faucet, you be wishing you were never born.

Isn't it wild when you say a word for the first time even though it's been in your mental vocabulary for years? And you're like, "am I saying this right? healthy? Is the *h* silent?"

***

The always chipper motherfuckers get on my nerves. If you don't experience some type of ennui or angst, you are either a key contributor to the lamentable facets of the human condition or purposely obtuse. I don't want to kick it with either.

***

You ever just scroll randomly through your phone contacts and think, *who the fuck is Leroy? When did I meet a Leroy? Why would I take the number of a Leroy?*

Yo, I wanna square up with whoever be writing these security questions for websites. The shits be mad unrelatable. "What is the name of the highest mountain you've climbed?" "What was your kindergarten teacher's blood type?" BITCH! I'm not tryna assassinate Oprah, I just wanna use your goddamn website for its services. One day I'm gonna be tryna to log into an account and be like "FUCK! How much did I weigh in the fifth grade?!"

***

Despite being blind as fuck, sometimes I'm in such an existential mood that I purposefully go outside without my glasses or contacts. I want these motherfuckers to be blurry; I don't wanna see them.

***

One of the most shocking truths when coming into adulthood is realizing how much fucking floor rugs cost. Three hundred dollars for some gotdamn fibers?! Bitch I think the fuck not. If I gotta piece together a bunch of bath mats like some struggle carpet, I guess that's what I'm finna do.

Ever been so poor that when you've gotten really sick, you waited until you've lost 6% of your body weight; then consequently started hallucinating before finally going to the ER? Then you hope you actually are dying; otherwise you're gonna be so mad if you get a bill for $5,000 only for the doctor to send you home with a recommendation of " just drink fluids." Nah doc, check the charts again. I got the bubonic plague. I better be dying. I ain't going into debt for a prescription of "stay hydrated."

***

If I gotta go to page two in a google search, that shit wasn't meant to be.

***

Dude: "do you work out?"
Me: "yeah."
Dude: "nice, what do you do?"
Me: "carry the weight of crushing existentialism."
Dude: "oh."

I don't answer the front door if someone is knocking and I'm not expecting a visitor. Previous generations would throw caution to the wind and answer the door all willy-nilly and end up deceased. Millennials could be two feet from the door while someone is ringing the doorbell and *still* not answer it. It could be the Secret Service and I'd still be shouting at a short distance, "THE FUCK YOU WANT?!"

***

You think you're self-confident until you have to help a fifth-grader with fractions.

***

I understand rideshare drivers are just trying to be polite in asking "you going to work?" when you get in their car, but how about you drop me off at 123 Mind Ya Business Boulevard? You got those coordinates my dude?

en you just finished paying at the cash ... and the cashier signals the next person to come over; yet you're still trying to put your money away, collect your shit and suppress your anxiety for not being quick enough. Like damn bitch can you wait until I've left the counter? I'm not an octopus; I only got two hands.

***

That feel when you spend 10 minutes typing a response to somebody's social media status; then you remember time is an illusion. Metaphysical solipsism postulates that the "external world" is merely an idea. "Real" is simply stimuli interpreted by the brain's nerve impulses. Life has no intrinsic meaning. Every living thing perishes and dissolves into nothing; so instead you hit delete and say, "never-fucking-mind."

***

The most devastating collection of words in the English lexicon: "now I'd like you all to separate into groups."

That feel when you try to hold in your cough in a public space because only two coughs are socially acceptable, but you can't. Then the public starts looking at you like you're about to resurrect an obsolete, infectious disease and you get self-conscious.

***

Seniors always be critiquing young body modified people like, "why you got all them holes in your face?" And you think, *why you got all them holes in your marriage? Don't start Mildred, I'll cancel your membership with AARP.*

***

(Gets brown rice on my 900 calorie burrito). (Whispers) "ah I'm healthy as fuck."

***

When you become woke:

Old friend: "Hey"

You: "New outlook who dis?"

Anytime a job post reads, "please send your cover letter" I'm like welp, looks like I'm not working there. I just spent *four* minutes updating my resume; I'm going to Jamba Juice, I've done enough.

***

You ever get frustrated watching these documentary-style reality shows where someone is like, "I'm Addicted to Shoving Dry Spaghetti Up My Butt." Yet they've somehow managed to find a partner who loves shoving dry spaghetti up *their* butt? But here you are still single; downloading and deleting dating apps every week and getting defensive when loved ones ask if you're "seeing anyone." And you're like, "I see someone everyday, I have vision."

***

I had a friend come over one day and he was knocking on my door and shit and I was like, "what is this 1952?" You text upon arrival binch. I hardly recognize a doorbell anymore; I assume it's a baby boomer's ringtone or the cops coming to arrest me for that tag I ripped off a mattress in 2009.

Y'all better be grateful we have google now 'cause there was a time when people had to go to the library for answers to ridiculous questions. You couldn't be at the microfiche smoking a blunt, eating Doritos and looking through peer-reviewed journals to answer why eleven isn't pronounced onety-one.

***

I got contacts with a brand new prescription and everything is so clear and like...significant. I'm so perturbed bitch I can't look people in the eye. I feel like I can see into the mailman's psyche. I can see my white blood cells. Oh my god, blurry is bliss.

***

That feel when you apply for hella jobs and an employer calls you back like, "you sent us your resume." And your scatterbrained, unemployed ass is like who the fuck is *us?* You've been eating nothing but long grain rice with roasted desperation and this binch is expecting you to remember *one* job outta 58 applications? BE SPECIFIC JULIE!

Wild Thots

In the African-American community, we don't say "wow you look really great!" We say, "BITCH SLAY ME, WHERE ARE MY EDGES? I'M BALD! STOMP ON ME! HOW DARE YOU! YOU JUST GON' FUCK ME UP LIKE THIS? HOW DISRESPECTFUL!" And I think that is truly beautiful.

***

If you still wear bootcut jeans, I know you don't hear it enough but you matter.

DMV agent: "eye color?"

Person with light eyes: "Well, when standing in the umbra of a shadow on a sunny day, they give off the appearance of chartreuse bespeckled with bits of sienna brown. However, under the night sky when the moon is at apogee, they look of the same green as the moorlands of Scotland."

DMV agent: Um okay. Go off I guess.

***

"Millennials are killing the wine industry."
"Millennials are killing department stores."
"Millennials are killing food chains."

If we are so good at killing, why y'all hatin' ass baby boomers still alive? You're still breathing (barely) as you dig into your lean cuisine, planning Bingo night with Susan and finding new ways to criticize younger generations. Don't be mad at us 'cause you can no longer buy your favorite orthopedic shoes at Sears. We stand quietly behind you in the convenience store line while you spend ten minutes buying lottery tickets with nickels; but y'all always running ya gums at us 'cause we can't buy a house.

All these people talkin' about "Jesus take the wheel." You sure about that? There were no automobiles during the Roman Empire, seems very irresponsible

***

Sometimes I think about how hip-hop is typically the only genre of music where if artists have beef, they release diss tracks. Then I think about what it would be like if other genres did that. Like what if Bon Iver and Mumford & Sons had beef? I'm just imagining white dudes who look like extras in *There Will Be Blood*, roasting each others' waistcoats and mutton chops and shit. And they'll be like, "your banjo ain't fair trade and you smell like cheroots/Are you even indie dude/Are those Kenneth Cole boots?/Your girl sucked my dick and we indulged in a multitude of sins/She told me you're a poser/That ain't even an authentic mandolin."

***

It ain't a real airport if it doesn't have a McDonald's. If I can't stuff my face with an overpriced McGriddle to help me forget my financial failures, I ain't fuckin' with it.

Listen, "all natural" products be cute and all but some of that shit don't be doing what it promises. A crystal ain't gonna clear my skin. A squeeze of lemon ain't gonna rid the shower of grout. You got me fucked up. Gimme the chemicals. Folks out here like, "suck on a sugar cube to prevent menstrual cramps." Fuck outta here! The healthiest people still be dropping dead at 50 and went through life smelling like must and oregano for nothing. Leave me and my chemicals alone. At least I'll have glowing skin and smell like an artificial summer breeze when I "shuffle off this mortal coil."

***

Your friend will be telling you a story and be like, "I was at the park with Roger..." and they literally never mentioned the name Roger before. They just gon' slide that name in the conversation without a subsequent description of who he is like you're supposed to know. Who the fuck is Roger? Your friend? Your gimp? Your weed man? A dog? If you tell me a story, I need you providing detailed prose like you're motherfuckin' J.K. Rowling; I wasn't there.

I used to think humans were superior to insects, but after spending three days trying to gain access into the psyche of a housefly, I've changed my tune. After many failed attempts of setting traps—and overestimating my fitness level in trying to swat—I eventually negotiated terms with it by offering it an Uber promo code to flee my room.

***

That feel when you just want your ride share driver to shut the fuck up while they drive you to your dick appointment but they keep runnin' their mouth. Then another passenger gets in engaging them in some bullshit about real estate and you like "E tu, Brute?"

***

Dudes who be like "I'm kind of a weirdo" really be thinking they're surfing some different wave of existence. Bring up nihilism and they start acting brand new. We've all heard Radiohead's "Creep" and got a stash of SSRIs, you ain't special. Talkin' about "normal people scare me." If you don't take your thumb ring and slouchy beanie wearing ass somewhere and go talk to an Amish girl on Rumspringa who might be impressed.

I hate when music elitists criticize pop music you have an attachment to 'cause you grew up listening to it. I'm sorry I wasn't intellectual enough to listen to conceptual rock on limited edition vinyl when I was 10.

***

I really be bothered when a cashier asks "how are you?" and I answer then reciprocate the question and they say nothing; scanning my items with a vacant stare. I know capitalism got you dead inside, but I wanna know how you are Carol? YOU STRESSED? YOU DEPRESSED? YOU THINKING 'BOUT A MCCHICKEN? DID YOU BUSS IT OPEN LAST NIGHT FOR THE NEW MANAGER? TELL ME!

***

Millennials out here so devoted to the zodiac that they'd be in court using their own horoscope as a defense. They be like, "now your honor; I couldn't have committed this *alleged* crime 'cause the New York Post said Mercury joined the sun in my Aquarius that week so I was at peace."

Most indie rock sounds like the manifestation of gentrification. An opening track plays, and if you listen carefully you can hear an artisanal mayonnaise shop being constructed softly behind the ironic accordion and soft boy vocals.

***

You ever retake insignificant personality quizzes that have absolutely no real world relevance simply 'cause you don't like the results? Fuck you results, I'm a peach not an avocado! What I gotta do to be a peach?

***

Climate Change is real bruh. Winters are getting hotter. Watch, next Christmas Santa gonna roll through ya crib with his beard shaved and basketball shorts on. He gonna be like, "fuck a milk 'n cookies fam, you got a Slurpee and a church fan?"

Man: (jizzes on towel).

Media: *Meet the Fresh New Artist Revolutionizing the Way We View Towels.*

***

It really disturbs me when people say "I don't care if you're black, white, brown or blue!" It should concern you to see a blue person. That either means they've stopped breathing or the aliens have finally invaded. You see a blue human, you call 911 or the Pentagon.

***

So homosexuality is a sin but we just gonna overlook jeans with no back pockets?

***

People who still type "www" before a web address are so precious like wow, vintage.

Why when you're prompted to input your date of birth on a website do they even have the current year as an option? Like, (pops out the womb and joins tinder) "I'm tryna fuck bitches! Where tha pretty hoes who know some good lullabies and an accredited pediatrician?"

***

People who have all white linens on their bed are wild courageous. Y'all on some next level shit and have reached an adulting milestone I can only dream of. I would have old ketchup stains and forgotten false lashes all up on them sheets. You're the real MVPs.

***

If you change the gender in love songs to match the gender you're attracted to when singing; you're a lil' bitch. You'll never survive the winter and natural selection gon' get you.

Hypermasculine dudes be like:

Deodorant: Lion-hearted body odor stick.
Razor: Macho multi-blade instrument.
Energy Drink: Real nigga beverage stimulant.
Stay-at-home dad: my dick juice made a kid and now I take care of it at the crib, masculinely.

***

I swear there is nothing more passive-aggressive than a mom washing dishes after cooking dinner but denying help. She says, "oh no, that's ok I've got it" but she be scrubbing them plates all mad.

***

People who say "I hate drama" remind me of how the Teenage Mutant Ninja Turtles would put on trench coats and fedoras to try and disguise the fact that they weren't human; however, their green turtle limbs would still be visible. We see your big ass turtle toes Raph, drop the masquerade.

People with naturally clear skin be like "I just cleanse my face with the wind and exfoliate with dirt hehe."

***

When you hit *input* on your TV remote, it's over bruh. You might as well throw the whole TV away.

***

Why everybody who shares screenshots have like 4% battery life? The tea that important you can't charge before you spill?

***

The Olympic Winter Games should recruit new athletes on the set of *Maury*. The way those guests be running, jumping and flipping when they realize they are "not the father" could easily earn the U.S. gold.

***

You *really* an actor if you've never been on *Law & Order: SVU*?

I don't know why older generations are always criticizing millennials and our use of technology. If it wasn't for us, they would still be spending $49.99 on rusty ass VHS porn; spending an excruciating 10 minutes fast-forwarding, tryna get to their favorite part so they can bust that nut. They should be grateful.

***

Servers in French restaurants be lookin' at you like you slandered Jean-Luc Godard when you ask for ketchup with your steak-frites. Listen, if I'm paying $30 a plate I need you to bring the Heinz without the 'tude chienne.

***

Some dudes really be exaggerating the volatility of their lives talkin' about "fuck all my adversaries." Adversaries my guy? You ain't Son Goku. You don't have a nemesis, you work at a warehouse.

Bruh, some of y'all need to think before you act. Don't ruin a life. Ask your friends before tagging them in a photo. Folks be snappin' shots not knowing ya angles and using harsh, undiffused flash then post that shit on social media with no regard. Got a bitch lookin' busted and spiraling into body dysmorphia.

***

I guess waifs are really feeling left out now that being "thick" is the wave. Bishes built like Audrey Hepburn be on the 'gram arching their back after eating some hot wings talkin' about "thiccums." You ain't thick though! You ain't thick, you bloated. Take some Beano and have a seat.

Memoirs of a Gangsta

Everyone wanna be "boujee" now. But when I drink $4 seltzer water out of a lapis lazuli goblet while writing down the best wine and cheese pairings in an artisanal leather journal; I'm "doing too much" and "being extra."

***

So happy I no longer measure my worth by the ability to make an origami crane.

At what age will I stop crossing the street when I see a group of trendy youths?

***

When characters have bad wigs and chapped lips in TV and film, I really get taken out of the narrative. They can afford exquisitely tailored costumes and sophisticated CGI, but the wig budget looks like it was $8 and the lips are crumbling like ancient ruins?! That shit is inexcusable bruh, chapstick is like $2!

***

I hate when I'm just tryna mind my own business and stream a movie illegally; as a result, a pop-up appears asking if I want to live chat with busty Russian bitches. The fuck I look like? If y'all had solid targeted advertising you'd know I prefer my busty bitches Hungarian. Nice try Annushka.

I don't know how some folks maintain so many relationships. I know a lot of people but have like three friends, and that's legit plenty. How some peeps be meeting Terry for breakfast, Oliver for lunch and Veronica for dinner is beyond me. I be confusing friends' hoe stories ("was it Marcel who fucked the born-again Christian?"), forgetting their new partner's names and mixing up brunch dates and shit.

***

One time this woman asked me if I had gotten a nose job, and I thanked her for thinking I have money.

***

If you gaze at me for an excess of five seconds, you better be prepared to ask for the link to my Amazon wishlist or fall in love with me.

***

When I hear people call guacamole "guac," I literally perceive it as an act of violence, take off my earrings and proceed to square up.

If you don't see color, how are you going to describe me to the sketch artist after I beat your ass?

***

I'm a strong, independent woman. If I can't open a jar I don't ask a man, I just throw the jar away. Fuck marinara.

***

I swear the next time an elderly person looks at my septum piercing with disgust talkin' about "did it hurt?" I'm gonna say "did it hurt when you fell and couldn't get up?" Try me Gertrude.

***

Me being a bitch: hmm thanks, you can't get it anymore it's vintage.

From time to time, I'll be having a conversation with someone and use a word I don't often use. Minor panic will set in because I'm unsure if I used the word correctly. So while the other person is talking, I'll take my phone out on the low and google the definition of the word and whisper "yes!" to myself when it turns out I was right.

***

I swear I hate calling businesses with a complex issue 'cause my ability to articulate goes straight out the window. I'll be like "so can you help me with my account...uh...uh such as the like such as" (insert nervous chuckling and an overwhelming use of "um"). I'm a millennial, if I can't text it, live chat it or discuss it over bottomless mimosas, I don't want to engage in it. It's 2018, we all have anxiety and a stash of benzos.

***

I'm sorry but moths unsettle the fuck outta me. Them niggas always flying around like their internal GPS is malfunctioning. Watch where the fuck you going B, this is a lace front.

Boycott Feelings

I have become so jaded from internet dating that I don't even try to present myself as charming or elusive on profiles anymore. I'm just like: I can form full sentences, my blood pressure is 130/80, let's fuck?

***

I'll be watching a crime show and the cops are chasing the perp and be like, "he's heading northwest on 2nd Street!" and I be thinking *I woulda lost that nigga. I'm not a Boy Scout bitch! I don't know cardinal directions. Is he behind the Panera Bread or not?! No time to take out a compass he's getting away!*

I don't understand why I'm single; I really don't ask for a lot. All I want is someone to dull the endless moments of existential dread, in which I question the purpose and value of my own existence; alleviate my chronic dysphoria; supply consistent life changing orgasms; and cook me hand-glazed black cod with a Japanese tamari and manuka honey reduction. Is that too much to fucking ask?!

***

Why do people put childhood photos on their dating profiles? As far as I'm concerned, you were never a child. You were born an adult; now you're dicking me down after three hours of whiskey drinking and extended gazes. I really don't need to be reminded of Picture Day in the 6th grade Tommy.

***

Your #MCM asks mixed girls "what's your nationality?"

You ever just look at a couple and think, *what the fuck do y'all talk about?* Their whole relationship is just a collection of "wyd?," "word?" and "mhmm's" and you just like, *how the fuck did these dry ass exchanges translate into a romantic relationship?* Don't even got opinions on polarizing shit:
—"You like pineapple on your pizza?"
—"Yeah."
That be the whole damn conversation. All these boring motherfuckers do is kiss and get smoothies. These reticent ass bitches finding love off one-word replies while Carl the Conversationalist is crying into his soup bowl, sad and single.

***

That feel when they're dope in every way possible but gotta corny name. You be conflicted, tryna figure out if you can say "FUCK ME HARDER MORTIMER!" for the next three years.

***

Some people regard meeting their partner's parents as a milestone in their relationship. Not me. Fuck parents. What are you going to play when I hand you the aux cord blud? 'Cause if that playlist ain't fire we're through.

Internet dating is like putting your music library on shuffle. The moment it starts playing you skip over every song; eventually getting so irritated 'cause you can't find a song you want to hear so you're like fine; it's 8 a.m. but I guess I'm listening to DMX.

***

Woman: "hey."

Straight dude: "Idk I just like...have a lot going on. I just got out of a long-term relationship four years ago and I'm just not ready to jump back into commitment. The sex was absolutely biblical, though. If you ever want to fool around again, you've got my number. In the interim—before I inevitably send you the "hey stranger" text, fuck the soul outta your body, then ghost you—don't be surprised if you see me on various dating apps seeking a partner in crime."

***

That feel when you've been single for so long that when someone asks you, "what's your type?" you respond with, "sans serif?"

One of my biggest fears of dating in San Francisco is going home with a date and realizing they own a unicycle.

***

Conversations with straight dudes be like:

Him: "Can I have your number?"
Her: "I have a boyfriend."
Him: "So we can't shower together as friends?"

***

Y'all fellow millennials better stop with this "let's grab a drink" bullshit. Does avocado toast get you through the whole day? Asking people out during dinner time straight after work, but we're sippin' on whiskey all night? Am I supposed to snack on conversation while you dig into your joke arsenal and discuss your hobbies? Bitch I'm hungry! I will not be giving the suck up on an empty stomach, I NEED TO EAT!

You ever start dating someone and your friends are like "show us what they look like," but you know they ain't photogenic. You be stressed as fuck, scrolling through their social media feed tryna find a decent pic thinking *he might just be ugly*; otherwise you know you about to get roasted for eternity.

***

I'm tired of straight men talkin' about wanting to meet a woman to "build him into a better man." I'm not tryna find a Build-a-Bear boyfriend or put bae together like a DOMBÅS wardrobe from IKEA. I'm not a general contractor my dude. You can show up a flawed human being, but don't expect me to correct your imperfections. Don't put it on me to be responsible for you becoming who you want to be. Taking control of *you* is called being an adult, get familiar.

***

Your #MCM replies "idk you just different" when you ask him why he likes you.

I really don't play around and chase people like I'm motherfucking Wiley Coyote. If they start to disappear and text one word responses and shit during the "courting phase," it's over bruh. Not only will I hit them with the "who dis?" text when I inevitably delete them from my phone, but I will delete their face from my memories on some *Men in Black* shit. Even in a lineup I'd be like, "I'm sorry detective I just don't see the one who had me fucked up." Too many times motherfuckers had me as the elective and not the court curriculum; I don't play that shit. Show me I matter right away or it's going to be a no from me dawg.

***

I'd rather be condemned to a life of wearing LEGO shoes than ever catch feelings again.

Send Nudes

Porn is getting really didactic. I was watching a video that involved a delinquent tenant and her horny landlord. I was thoroughly educated on renters' rights more than any seminar I've ever attended and *still* got my nut. This is why duality was invented.

***

I hate when straight men don't moan and stay hella quiet during sex. Aye, we fuckin' or recording an ASMR video? I need you screeching at a frequency so high that a colony of bats fly to the bedroom. I need you hitting that falsetto, stop playin'.

Thirsty dudes be like:

Lissen shorty, I'd adopt a life of asceticism and relocate to the Himalayan mountains; eating nothing but yak cheese, with only a distressed pair of 11's to my name just to sniff the inside of your bra. And you gotta give these niggas credit for their creative prose.

***

If you were never convinced that America is over-sexualized, just watch a commercial. Why the fuck are they out here personifying and sexualizing food?! They got chocolate candies wearing falsies. Pastries speaking all breathy. Waffles with legs, crossing them all lasciviously like it's Sharon Stone in *Basic Instinct.* I want to eat the food not smash the granny out of it. There is no need to make a piece of chocolate flirtatious. The shit is already good and getting eaten regardless. Y'all need to chill.

***

Me to myself when I'm trying not to be a hoe:

He has the dick you deserve, but not the one you need right now.

Dudes be rubbing on ya clit all aggressive like they tryna summon a sleeping genie.

***

I never get lonely cos there's always busty MILF's in my area who wanna chat.

***

I don't sleep in the nude to be more comfortable, I sleep in the nude so my body is always ready. I never know if the ghost of Bruce Lee will decide to haunt my bedroom. Well Bruce, yank off those covers so you can haunt this pussy!

***

It's 2018. If you ain't eating my ass, tagging me on memes and praising my eyebrows, we don't have a future.

Me: "You eat ass?"

Him: "Nah."

Me: "Why don't you get back to your lil' cathode monitor, waiting for your Napster file to download and contact me when you grow up you dial-up modem ass bitch!"

***

Why do so many dudes laugh when trying to initiate sexting? Y'all be like, "what would you do if I was there? Haha." Haha? Haha? You wanna see these titties or not my dude? We tradin' nudes or knock-knock jokes?

***

If it's not ok for people to get paid for sex why do we call so many sex acts "jobs?" Hand *job*, blow *job*, rim *job*. Binch fill out that 1099 form and clock that ass in.

If I start sleeping with you and you ask for a nude, just know that you're most likely getting a recycled one that somebody else has seen. If you text me and I'm lying in bed watching Netflix and eating Hot Cheetos, you better believe I'm not getting up. I'm not going to spend 10 minutes trying to find a sensual angle for my ass when I gotta finish *Peaky Blinders*. My nude office hours vary weekly. You will accept my nudes; whether they're my ass from last week or last year. Be grateful and get your nut. Now send me that dick dawg.

***

I'll get hit with some struggle dick and subsequently turn into wanton Goldilocks, tryna find the dick that's just right like her warm porridge. Weak stroke game is like watching a three-hour movie with no plot developments and an ambiguous ending. I ain't finna end the week on an unsatisfactory note after I filled out the time sheet and put in the work. Nah, if you ain't gonna give me my orgasm I'll go searching for it on some carnal adventure like I'm Jonny Quest.

Who told y'all that telling somebody—"I'm gonna blow ya back out," "I'm gonna fuck you so hard you can't walk," "I'm gonna split you in two," "Ima be up in your guts"—you're about to have sex with, that that is sensual? That's not sensual to me. Am I about to get dicked down or audition for the next installment of *Saw*? You're gonna fuck me into paralysis? Are you gonna pay my bills while I'm bedridden and call outta work? Is there an EMT on standby? I like dick but it ain't worth the risk of muscle atrophy.

***

Straight dudes are always saying, "man I love pussy." You love pussy huh? Name five of their albums. Were you there when Pussy was playing $5 shows? Do you even have the *Cunnilingus Mixtape* with the hidden bonus tracks: "Give Me An Orgasm" and "Don't Forget the Clit" (produced by MC Lickety Lick)? Yeah that's what I thought.

I have absolutely no patience. If a Pornhub video stops buffering I just throw the whole computer away.

***

That feel when you're on public transportation and open your browser to google airfare, but "busty babe needs a dick to distract her" starts playing.

***

When people tell me to curse less, smoke less, and be less vulgar; I'm just like well damn, just slap the dick outta my hand too. Can a bitch live? Can a heaux breathe? Can a diva exist?

Have You Tried Not Being Depressed?

Sometimes I'll be so eager to bounce back from a depressive episode that I'll eat one vegetable and go 45 minutes without self-loathing and be like, "depression? I don't know her. That was the old me, I'm a new bitch."

That feel when you smoke excessively; never eat veggies; drink two ounces of water a week; sleep on a dirty pillowcase; subsist on skittles and *still* get acne. Like wow, where is this coming from?

***

Mental illness memes have become so much the norm that when you say, "I'm mad suicidal bruh," your doctor be like, "me too bitch the fuck."

***

That feel when someone has the audacity to FaceTime you without making an appointment first. You just stare at the phone in awe 'cause you've been in the same depression clothes for three days straight, hair all disheveled; you haven't had at least three hours to conquer your body dysmorphia, beat your face and figure out a flattering lighting concept.

That feel when there's some news headline like "Asteroid Headed For Earth" and you get excited, but then there's a subtitle: "But Don't Worry, That's Just the Title of Michael Bay's New Film." Then you're just like wow, I was really ready to "shuffle off this mortal coil" how dare you mislead me this way.

***

That feel when you go out despite your chronic depression; start dissociating at the function; get ready to leave, but you hear "cash money taking over for the '99 and 2000" so you stay and delay your melancholy for 3 minutes and 51 seconds.

***

So many online dating profiles talk about "let's go on adventures" and I'm thinking: *I won't bungee jump in Switzerland but I cut my own bangs during mental breakdowns and frequently dissociate. Ain't a bigger risk taker than me my dude, now suck my titties and tell me I'm loved.*

Not to toot my own horn but I make poor life decisions *without* the influence of alcohol. We can't all be legends.

***

That feel when your anxiety is at odds with your desire to adopt a chill, online aesthetic. You want to ignore grammar rules and punctuation but you out here panicking at self-made typos.

***

Why sleep when I can dissociate for eight hours?

***

My kink is thinking about some embarrassing shit I said in the eighth grade.

K byeee

Send all inquiries to:

info@marquitanorwood.com

Social Media

Facebook: @justmarquitathings
Instagram: @marquitasade
Twitter: @marquitasade

Customized china featured in author's photo:

Bad Wolffe Vintage
Instagram: @badwolffe_vintage

Made in the USA
Columbia, SC
11 August 2018